Sonnets
of various sizes

Peter Oswald

Sonnets
of various sizes

Shearsman Books

First published in the United Kingdom in 2016 by
Shearsman Books
50 Westons Hill Drive
Emersons Green
BRISTOL
BS16 7DF

Shearsman Books Ltd Registered Office
30–31 St. James Place, Mangotsfield, Bristol BS16 9JB
(this address not for correspondence)

www.shearsman.com

ISBN 978-1-84861-492-5

Contents

In a letter, Hopkins wrote that the English sonnet is too short, because Italian vowels are longer than English vowels, and the Italian is the original and perfect sonnet. So in this collection you will find one extended sonnet – Les Murray wrote that an example of 'sprawl' (which is something he approves of) is a sonnet in its twenty-first line. You will also find some sonnets from the Italian of Dante, crammed into tight English vowels. Some sonnets that don't rhyme. Some in the rhyming-couplet form of John Clare. And some poems of fourteen lines which are probably not sonnets at all.

(These poems were written over a period of thirty-two years. They are not arranged in chronological order.)

Love all at once – heart bursting into head,
Every not yet and now and finished instant:
Would crack the brain, like as if all the dead,
Future and past, and those dying this moment,
Sucked, great star-cloud, into a garden shed,
Or every rose-seed crammed into one case,
Growing one rose, with the whole world, its bed,
Squeezed in the talon roots. The human race,
Its final number, has to be outspread,
Like refugees on a long road, flung dots
Of difference, fields not murdered into bread;
And roses have to grow in separate spots;
And I have got to love you bit by bit:
Flashes of scraps, like windows headlight-lit.

As I went looking for my love,
On a wet bank I slipped – a stripe
Of damp on my left cheek, a swipe
From a low branch sagged in the wet
Of its dead freight, not dropped yet
Into the litterings that spread
Orange-brown circles, pools of shed
Prototype souls, or skins of thought
Not wrong but just used up. Hooks caught
Then, in the flapping of my jacket,
Sharp rose-memories, and my right boot
Sank, and I, reeling, dragged at it,
And sinking flailed and flailing sink
As through the wet wood weave my loose footprints.

My lover is like Berkshire in the night.
She stretches out like Slough beneath the stars.
Her veins are lamplit sidestreets where warm cars
Pass on a wave of light from light to light.
Between her towns dark woods bow to the moon,
But total darkness you will never find,
Always some vestige of the afternoon
Keeps shining like the daydreams of the blind.
She has some heaths where people never go,
Or if they do, at certain moonless times,
Think themselves ghosts revisiting their crimes,
And feel eternity's dead heart beat slow.
But just when she's convinced them that they're dead,
Morning gets up again in Maidenhead.

Love is a medical emergency,
Cell-overload of electricity,
Heavy intensifying mist of light
Mixing the mind's eye up with the eyesight.
A sudden swishing secrecy of screens,
A drunken disappearing of betweens,
And you are opened in a necessary
Ancient suspension of all modesty.
But you are two and this is a magician
Mending them in the mask of a clinician,
No, a witchdoctor with a smiling knife
Cutting towards the noose around your life,
As it hangs in the balance. First in crisis
Joins us, and then in crisis separates us.

(Wedding present)

That was the day the sun just went on rising
Into the light; the thrush, in its dawn singing,
Out-topped its highest note until unheard ones
Shattered the windows of the chapel and
Of the skyscrapers flashing tangerine,
And the glass flew straight up into the stars;
Mercury burst from the barometers
In bullet streaks; tall-stretching sycamores
Were pumas sharpening their branchy claws
On the sky's ice; hawks shrank into the stratosphere,
Mountains grew mountains as if bodybuilding –
And the most near pressed close to the most far.
Then the whole thing snapped shut with a string's twang
Into this silver locket – here you are.

Closest, I recognise her least. She breaks,
Glass of a river when it melts through rocks,
Shatters into a crowd of characters,
Dark glitterers and silent chatterers,
All of her selves, all her past lives, her strata,
Orange leaving dashing to a brink of water,
All claiming this one moment, shades who crowd
To the trench filled with honey and hot blood,
Slowed by Odysseus with his blade, lost man
Hardened to make them answer one by one.
Who are you when you are a swarm of bees,
Split from the hive, between localities,
Who, when the next is found, sink back unseen
Into the sleeping person of the Queen?

(Vows)

This is no shapeless patch of territory.
We travelled here by random roads for certain,
but it's a place, it is a certain country,
and we have earned a certain recognition,
since it was us who chanted out the borders,
marking the flowing map of what we move in.
So the dark field I climb is you, the village
beyond, in rising light, all have love's features.
Which are a cage of light to free the eyes,
or water to the seal released, who touches
at every stroke, no edge, no see-through limit
with faces pressed against. So he abandons
triangulating fear with death and failure,
and hate's co ordinates all prove inaccurate.

Carrying one another carefully
Over the stones, each brimful of the other,
And careful not to spill, exchanging spoonfuls,
Like children feeding one another medicine –
Be careful how this concentration
On the midpoint, leaves free the fringe of vision
For half-seen things to enter, bright invasion
Not border-checked by thoughts, but flooding
As through the eyes of leafless Eve and Adam,
Accumulating insect-jewels, feather-crowns
That will be hard to carry later on.
Beware you bearing one another's bones,
Like flowers, the later limping over stones,
Laden with treasures and without a helper.

She's somewhere in the house. I will not go
To find her, right now. Let her be alone,
We will meet later, so I can be slow,
Not even bother with the phone,
Or shrieking of a child or animal,
Unless insistent. I will often stir
For no good reason, she is beautiful,
Focus my vacant gaze to look for her,
As if love was a novel I was loving,
Left in the wrong place, under towels or something,
And it concerns me, it will tell my ending,
Like the sky's flying fires. But for the time being,
Let her be everywhere, fill all the rooms
With various possible sweet and bitter dooms.

In all this grass there is no other hare,
Only you swerve around me everywhere,
Your movements started by my movements, mirror,
Shadow more real than me, thrown on the water
That swerves around me, shadow cast on air.
Beyond the end, the cows are interesting,
In their own way, the pigeon shards that fling
Out of the big beech trees. The trees are stranger -
Tall heifers grabbing hay out of a manger,
They snatch the wind. But there is nothing here
Other than you, we move in the same fear:
My death, your death. Then, at the end of danger,
Only this grass, only, to fill the mirror,
The stirring of the air and of the water.

My something love, when the dark's hair is down,
and trees are whispered rumours of the end,
but the idea of day begins to dawn –
over the plough, blind, feeling for your bones
hidden among the flints, you go, and skim
your skin from off the brambles' slag of crowns,
that are beginning to begin to sing –
badger around, baglady-gathering
liver and heart and lungs – you fish your tongue
out of a ditch – now you are looking for
your eyes, now you have found them on a stone,
now day's train's coming and you rush to plumb
all this together in a tight space, perfect
for shadow-throwing when the light is outright -

Like walkers passing one another soaking
From the same downpour in the cloudy mountains,
Their coats all shining eyes, their bright mouths joking
About a ramble through the Trafalgar Square fountains,
From time to time we look at one another
And laugh. How did I get to be a father;
How did you, hushed girl, come to be a mother?
When both for certain at one time would rather
Have been tall trees divided by deep water?
Now our eyes meet across a kitchen table
Wrecked by the storm of two sons and a daughter,
And we exchange as much as we are able –
An escalator glance – or else a shiver
As when the neck's drips tickle the spine's river.

Daughter, the streets have snatched you and the screens
Of shops and all the life of widening eyes –
From the one avenue of wise beech trees
I carried you along, you strapped to me,
Asleep, then sitting on my hip, astride,
And pointing to the shriek and after-scare
Of birds I pointed out. A blur of days
Has whirled you like a shotput with the speed
Of the sun chasing its own tail, sun-hungry,
And flung you blazing deep into the starlight.
A shiver in the corner of the mirror
Is you, then gone, and I am following,
A fading ghost, or silver moon-sliver
That lifts into the laughter of the weather.

Cold May comes through the window – trembling panes
Have marked its passage through the glass and through
The water of our glances, down the lanes
Of lungs, trees shaken by its nowhere blue.
A glimpse of its no-face where cloud-thoughts pass
Through its unmind, will wipe your face away,
A finger-picture on the misted glass,
And put you in its place, so that cold May
Is staring out at you. See where it stares
Out at you now, two children eating toast,
Normally noisy, but now hushed as hares:
Cold May has filled them with its shivering ghost,
And you must change and come back to them soon,
With all the shouting sunlight of warm June.

Over the pub roof words like seeds come flying
Into our heads, out through our mouths, leap over
To the far bank, or drop into the river
And curve away into cold light forever.
Now the wind drops, and our slack heads are resting
On the slight interruption, or are climbing
Back up the path to where we were all standing
On the cliff-edge, like a rook inquest gabbling
About the drop, and the black water glimpsing
Through the steep trees. And now the words come running
To catch us up, we are one moment summer
Dry, the next moment full and rushing winter,
Seasons pass through us quicker than the swallow
Under the eave and out, too fast to follow.

Bales of scrap gold. There is no other word
In sunlight to describe them. So you leap
Off them, and fall, wing-steadied like a bird
Of prey feet forwards whoosh into a heap
Of feathers and a dust-burst. And you stare
All afternoon at stars that bulge up there,
Through pinholes in the corrugated rust
Roof. There are pits down which you can descend
As if down chimneys. There might be no end
To that profoundment but there is. You must
Stop, till your breath comes quiet in the strawed
Shaft. And they blink, but cannot see you there,
Where you sit thinking sunk deep in your chair
About the barns in which these days are stored.

Like a wood pushing through a wood, a carpet
Lifting another pattern through its pattern,
Or the face in a portrait painting fading
As a new face behind it starts to brighten,
And drinks its pigments and invades its features,
This is the coming generation,
The next wave moving through us, where we're lying,
Scattered, some dead, some dug in, others raving
On the barbed wire, a few in shellholes calling
Encouragement. But these are not our comrades,
These reinforcements stepping through the dead ground
That we have gained – though allies they are foreign,
Grunt as they pass through our weak-held position
Towards objectives secret from our briefing.

A whale sings deep inside your stomach, wakes
Messengers who now struggle through your guts
With squelching steps. Down here dawn never breaks,
Unless a surgeon or a murderer cuts.
Your heart, a sunken sack of letters, sags,
Rising and falling in the the pulsing flood,
Gesturing weakly like the signal flags
Of a sunk frigate. Ciphers in the blood
Rise almost wordlike almost out of it,
Scurrying just beneath the surface. Bread
Is good to buy the silence of this pit
About the date it plans to wake you dead,
Though still you strain to glean from the declensions
Of soft suspended bells, the deep's intentions.

We who will not die stand beside a stone,
Talking about a piece of finger bone
That one of us is holding in his hand,
Joking he knows who it belonged to, and
He says her name, perhaps made up. We laugh,
And the duckpond takes a flash photograph.
And she who did not die, though she did see
A thin old woman gaping endlessly
On a cold bed, who she could almost name
(But then all old dead people look the same,
Even yourself,) she joins us, like a sigh.
We who will not die, she who did not die,
Smile at the pipe-end of her finger bone,
Then put it back and set back up the stone.

How can we wake you up? You sleep so well,
After the all-day hospital radio,
Tuned out of tractors and of gulls and blackbirds.
Clearly no steaming elephant parade
With naked ladies on snorting horses,
And acrobats, will do it, nor the clowns
Cartwheeling, clearly all these things will fail,
As will the shrill commands of sergeant-majors.
Quiet will maybe touch you, so we go
Quietly by you, speaking soft and low,
Like breathing summer trees. Or in some countries,
Spread out a picnic, eat all over you,
Tempting you with cheese triangles. But no,
You are not drawn to us as we to you.

(The dead)

Some rush straight off to speak to Socrates.
Some huddle, like a shape of smoke or steam
Struggling to keep its shape, with arms of steam
Or smoke. Some find a corner to sweep clean,
And here the dust is truly infinite,
And the day not shaped by television.
Their whistling drips into unbottomed cisterns
That echo empty. You lose everything:
Lead snaps, dog long-tongues off into the distance
And disappears, skirts trail long threads, unhemmed,
Edges are rumoured, borders merely hummed –
People soon leave, in drips and drips, like water
From the cold windows of its condensation
To the warm floor of its ascension falling.

Bells running over their beads, over the hills
Carrying water, now the water spills,
Drops down eight steps, now down eight steps the same,
Like children chanting in a chanting game,
Over and over. Who are they in there,
Pressing their repetition on the air,
Against its fading saying it again,
Like a wren singing that it is a wren?
They must be true and honest, clear and free,
To issue such a depthless melody,
Unchangingly extended. But my ear
Picks out the gaps, the little blanks of fear,
Glues them into a flute, church-tower-strong,
Which plays for me my own deathsong.

Actually skeletons are not bad looking,
Clear cheekbones, endlessly inward glances –
Sprawling in shallow pits they are still striking,
Negligent arm behind the head, legs scissored,
Or tucked up foetus-like, this anti-foetus,
That asks no answer from the mind,
Much like a multi-storey carpark.
Skeletons are not horrible,
It is these heavy overhangings,
Ripping and hopelessly re-stitching,
These screaming seeds, these orbs tight-swelling,
These aching sacs. So much soft stuff squashed in!
This is the bruise, this is the stain
That blots the beauty of the skeleton.

Owlshriek: scrape of a sword withdrawn
From stone flesh on the field of the frozen.

Dogbark answer: the echo (distorted)
Of spring laden with laden drones.

Sycamore: seethe of the sea stripped down
To a bone hand sticking out of the ground.

Rain in the beech hedge: sleet on shingle;
The stunned wave breaks straight through the closed room.

Ice in the earth's core dripping, hissing;
Winter brings the antidote to spring.

Drain it at a gasp, feel the misery drain
First from your feet, then from your heart, then,

Join the dead in their teeth-set prone
Deep celebration of the dead season.

Poet, throw death out. If you do not throw him,
Since death is nothing, so will be this poem,
A catalogue of absences, a hymn
To a blocked lift-shaft or extinguished gym
Where the ballbaskets droop unflipped and white
Lines are not strobing in and out of sight
Under the braking twist and squeal of soles,
And there is no whitewater roar for goals.
Do not attempt to make your subject death.
Whoever wrote a sonnet with no breath?
Let your tight lines fish life straight out of life,
Flash like the sunlight biting on a knife
That spins so swift the blade seems to be bending.
Death will be dealt with, anyway, by the ending

A naked woman, lovely as the night,
Its beauty concentrated in the moon,
A woman made of moonlight, made of moons
Turning together, has got up and run
Out of the Zdolbunov ravine. Two men
Are walking through the women, shooting them,
Where they are lying naked on the ground,
Maybe two hundred, all in rows, face down,
Most of them dead already, one alive,
Half lifted on her elbow. But this one
Has ripped out of the photograph and run,
Growing with every stride up to the moon,
Treading the steppes, eyes level with the sun —
And runs forever and does not look down.

(Speech)

Out of their caves we came like echoes,
mimics, with nothing of our own to say.
These chanting springs, low mountains wandering,
black speaking swamps, have tacked the mothertongue
of earth to us, the burp of bogs, spat gravel,
white banshee scream of tundra wind – that turns
the air between us green with female meaning,
speech of the dead, earth in the mouth, word-potions
that change us, when we try to speak, to gravestones
naming the ground, all our upsoarings dampened
and riddled into mud. Men have no language,
all speech is female and we can say nothing.
Before they drag us back into their word-womb,
drive them back into the ravine they came from.

At last, the great Third Reich victorious,
All the vast east subdued and the tanned tent
Of every starving halfbreed trampled flat,
And the great swirl of jigsaw shades and shapes,
The jumbled Empire, the untidy States,
The worldwide autumn leafmap, swallowed up
By the sky drinking smoke with eyes shut tight,
Till they could open satisfied and bright
On a world-sky made clear by strong blue light –
There was a pause. Then the Creator stepped,
He formed himself in black and silent ranks,
Serenely gazing deep into the past,
A brambled forest cleared out and made waste,
And at a barked command he shot himself.

A fawn's been blinded by the birds. Beware,
There are so many of them in the air,
Feathered with darkness, which they want to share,
Pecking up scraps of shadow everywhere.
Or hungry for the light, straight for the eye
Stabbing, as if to eat a little sky,
Grinding it back to darkness in their gizzards.
I used to love their flocks, the big black blizzards,
Chaotic choirs, the opposite of quiet,
Sabring the blue to shreds with their high riot.
But now they make me count how many things
Love to eat eyesight. With or without wings,
Looking for something lost, to blind. Beware,
There are so many of them everywhere.

The forthright hawk, discussing with the dove,
Swiftly convinces. His hooked finger prods,
Proving his point, a sharp one from above,
From way above her soft head that now nods
In deep agreement. But he won't relent,
Tearing the carcase of her argument
Down to the melting marrow, not content
Till he has crammed her entire testament
Into his gullet. So she keeps conceding,
Feather by feather, string by strip of red,
Till her thin bones all shine, leeched of their pleading,
And all her thoughts have entered through his head
Into his blood, except for one fine-shaded
Question that drifts downwind, not quite persuaded...

There are no lions in the stubble fields,
Or in the woods, there are no dinosaurs
Crowding the lane, heavy with living shields,
Swinging their club tails, no red tiger roars
Near the stockpens, to cause a stir in the straw.
There are no crested reptiles in the air,
None in the trees, no elk-foot or wolfpaw
Presses the dust. But there is something there –
Here on the window-sill, a brown oak eggar,
Shivering, stirring up its strength, stiff fore-legs
Rubbing red eyes, that flash, each frond antenna
A feeling leaf. Brown-tented like tuaregs
That you approach, a shimmer in the distance,
Trembling and growing, trembling into instance.

Now day has exorcised the woods. The breeze
Polkas through ghostless groves, the trees are trees,
Light has reformed their off-world character
And chained them to the ground. Now go back where
You stood last night when you were jumped by fear,
Under twin limes trees, trying to find a thought
To disenchant the beech beside the gate
That you would have to pass, did pass, late late,
Muttering prayers, poor fool. Well it did work
A little bit, the lime leaves in the night
Scattered a little memory of light,
As now conversely they imply the dark,
Saying like midwives, breathe and breathe and push
Yourself out now through terror with a rush –

Whole-day-long journeys, hours of fields and towns,
Are being shrivelled into glimpses, named
Into small forms, like the entire South Downs
On a matchbox; whole nations snapped and framed
In miniature. Enormous rivers pour
Into a headset, city parks are stored
In stacks of discs, and the sands of the shore,
That can be neither counted nor ignored,
Are melted into a glass bead. Contained
By a small sacrifice of detail, all
The fragments of expanding matter rained
In through the eyes are packed down and stowed small
As the vast fires out at the edge of time,
Cradled in numbers or a nursery rhyme.

SUN
Moon
SUN
Moon
SUN
Moon
SUN
Moon
Balloon
Balloon
Balloon
Balloon
SUN
Moon

(The wind)

Having no mouth, I have to use the world,
Its polyp-fields of sea-swayed lungs that gape
And make me tiny in the tightly curled
Tightening spiral that's my briefest shape.
Having no blood, I have to spark what's there,
Heavy revolving liquid lost to light,
With the dead-feather-twitching gift of air,
Courting of aspens where the green turns white.
Having no thoughts, I have to storm your brain,
Blasting the thinkers out of their grey beds;
Having no coat to keep out my own rain,
I have to squeeze into your drabbling threads,
And run you flapping till I lie you still
As the cloud-leopard sleeping on the hill.

The clouds are copying the trees and cows
With all their might, as they pass over, strain
Against the wind's will, briefly to be boughs
Or bones. Distraction spins the weathervane,
But the clouds concentrate like children, trace
A map of the Americas or mime
Like clowns a marching army, make the face
That makes a face at them. And all the time
The houses and the horses on the ground
Are copying themselves, and have become,
Against the world's will, as it spins them round,
Almost exact – though in the struggle, some,
Have lost, like us, the key to their encryption,
Too roughly sketched to fit their own description.

Six foot of intricate machinery,
Fine-wired, is necessary just for me
To stand among the christened stones and see
And hear this blackbird in the old yew tree.
To think it blanks the screen immediately –
As if a man should kiss a woman and see
Behind her eyes, her entire ancestry
All standing in a line, near truth of skin
Only the engine of a time-long train,
Stretching right back to where the stars begin.
But now the springs and flywheels of the crane
That hoists me here, get back to work again –
Jammed for a blink in my own cogs, but then
Oiled and fine-tuned by the old song, the sweet strain.

Here is my hand, a future map they say,
Ordinance Survey of my destiny.
Into this parchment a cartographer,
At the dictates of an astrologer,
Pressed his thread lines, when I was in my mother,
Head down. They wander over one another,
This is a palimpsest, new roads marked bold
Over the fainter tracings of the old
Field boundaries and footpaths. Further back,
The broken contrail of a Saxon track,
Then nothing but the circlings of a hare
On the dry earth. So I have got nowhere,
Traveller through the prospect of a land
To the far-off horizons of my hand.

(Westminster Bridge)

Trickles of thinking mingle with the flow
From pipes invisible. On my left hand
Westminster bickers as the waters go
Carrying off the loose parts of the land.
This town will stain my ghost when I am gone
If I do not scour off into the brown
Flowers beneath my feet, all I have done,
Shake it off doglike, let it all go down
To join the squeezed-out city's boil of poisons,
Stirred to one colour by the rush to ocean,
Seepage released from cinemas and prisons,
Rainwater rainbowed from the roads' commotion –
Drain my whole mind, that the returning tide
Will bring me back, I hope, sea-bright, sea-wide.

One day a song will burst into my brain
Out of the murk of my own mystery,
So powerfully a moment's tune, the strain
Of a precise time, pitch of history
Specific to an instant, that – it might be
Radio something car dark-driven warm,
As if along the bottom of the sea,
With him and them and nothing of the storm
Over us – or some other song-fixed scene
Out of the swirling breaking suddenly
Into my mind's mind, rush of ocean green
So close it holds me, infinite High C,
Trapped in the circle of its harmony,
Like the ongoing echo of the sea.

Often I've tried to settle in this place,
And searching for a more-than-granite base
For my foundations, seized a line of music
Which by its loveliness – or else a face –
Might make perpetual repetition easy;
As if a man should snatch a dragonfly
Out of the air and on its back construct
A palace for his endless residence,
Or find a sea with breakers but no beach,
Where he could surf forever and not reach
Anything, carried on an inheld breath,
As on the awe of a vast audience,
Balancing on their not wanting to cough,
Without the need to rest by falling off.

Ladywell has gone up into the sky,
As if she never had been more than thin
Architect's lines, that with a Thursday sigh
Are scrunched and chucked into the paperbin.
She has been entered in the book of air,
Where queens are kneeling on a towered green,
The moon unwalked; whose pages cannot tear,
Printed in lines of light by what has been.
Her demolition has completed her,
Now she cannot be smashed by any hammer;
Diggers and skips have not defeated her,
Abstracted by the drill's pneumatic stammer.
But when will I be bold enough to roam
Her floating gardens, enter my old room?

David stood firm against a storm of days,
that battered him with roof-tiles, bricks and broomsticks.
An hour was longer than a week of rain
sometimes, the man inside a stuffed bird, caged –
heart winced up tighter than a fist, a foetus.
Then came a little golden age,
heralded by a dance – and then a wedding,
and hours were pearls all fitted to a string.
Where have they all gone now? The string has broken,
the pearls are scattered like the smile of morning
that a rainburst in the lunchbreak has punched out!
Look, here he comes now, up the road, bent forward
slightly, against the fall of man, amazed:
the shrub he cut back to its roots is roof-high!

Waiting for the renewal of my passport,
I had four hours to walk the streets of Newport,
Where the Usk thickens as the sea sucks out
The brown blood of the province. A loud shout
Might reach right down the High Street to the docks,
Where the cranes angle, hands of giant clocks –
A giant shout would do it. Here in chains
The High Street lies, a prone spine, the remains
Of a mediaeval beast. The Wednesday shoppers
Were searching for its heart, with shiny coppers
Laid on their eyes, not speaking their own language.
I dwindled to a pinhead, but a sandwich
Recovered me enough to fetch my passport
And pass again outside the bounds of Newport.

Elderly summer in her Ascot hat
Of heaped up flowers, is sitting on the grass,
And all around her everything's rained flat
And rain has wrecked the Soave in her glass.
Blue of her dress has soaked into her skin,
And tears whose cause she can't remember blur
Her turquoise eyelids. Ought she to go in?
The bursting horses bleeding from the spur
Have all turned into clouds, that slowly merge
Into each other. Surely everything
Is sliding to its wretched end, the verge
Of the flat earth, shrill with sheer trumpeting?
The bloody oil has drowned us finally!
Run to the flooded paddock of the sky!

(Sleep)

Fraying defence against tomorrow morning,
Thin ply of darkness, bread and butter buttress,
Slowing down time with timelessness, that lasts
No time at all – a scorched sky policy,
Brightening the earth. A tide of twittering
Will swamp your sandcastle of sleep with brightness,
Though you retreat a thousand miles inland,
Curl in the stone-crammed stomach of a stone,
Flick of a switch will fetch you back again,
Drag you across the sunrise Kalahari,
Protesting that you are a desert flower,
Splash you with ice-cold facts, and all day long,
Out of worn daylight you must patch again
Your thin defence against tomorrow morning –

(Spring)

The churchyard oaks and cherries have been stone
All winter long in sombre imitation,
As if it was their own sucked-in tradition,
This suited look, as self-contained as coffins,
This spare review in stone and brief summation –
A troop of children standing to attention
Outside the granite palace of the Ice Queen,
All through the cold war and the threatening heaven,
Grown-up as graves. Until a tickling wind
Grows a green grin – and then the next one, sensing
The silent spreading seismic crack, acquires one,
And then the next – and then a quivering
Chin – and then all of them are silently
Shaking, and now the whole platoon is howling –

Now summer in her loveliness is here,
I ask her will she join me for a beer
At the Stag's Head? She gets up very early,
Her eyes are blue, her hair is green and curly.
She tells me not to treat her like a lady,
She says my dealings would be far more shady
Under her trees. We try to make a time
To meet. She speaks non-sequiturs in rhyme.
She tells me in an accent of December
Not to be always trying to remember
The present. Now the talk is all of her
On the high hills, how in her lightest fur
She walks among the gorse. She has three names.
I call them out and she bursts into flames.

Rain falling out of heaven hurriedly,
Stripping the peeling sky of its dampstains,
With deep concern for the dry leaves that wave
A wilting signal of emergency –
Sinks to the driest inmost coil
So it snaps open – even to the brain,
Old dusty wasp's nest hanging in a tree,
Buzzing again and dark with sharpest honey.
So God is made of water obviously,
Falls, pools – the shifting big locality
Of vastest beasts in deepest deeps set free,
Torrents and wild spouts twisting to the sky,
Tending to clouds, but drifting down again,
Easing the paths of snails, the ways of seals

Now listen in to the periphery,
The fringe of sound, that's neither mine nor me,
The foreign English language of the pigeons.
Widening down from green and lifted regions,
Swerving around and up, with different rhythms
Rippling the lower and the upper fathoms.
Not lovers talking quietly and closely,
Sway-walking, two who are one body loosely
Tied at the arms. Not traffic at the junction,
Not the airwaves where you might get a mention,
Not children whispering or the talk of actors
Tumbling, not the light-brushstroke talk of doctors.
Not, not – by means of nots the tangled mind
Flaps free of netting and rejoins the wind.

The wind that shakes the ilex tree shakes me,
The glare that blanks the stars wills me awake.
Across a paving stone across the sea,
The leaf that shuffles crablike for my sake,
Opens my eyes and wipes mist from the lake.

But still it shakes as though stung to be free,
And now the later light caught by my eye,
That strains to read the number of a psalm
Over a dead man's shoulder, makes it calm,
In obedience to the solemnity of the sky.

This is a jewel I take out sometimes,
When all but one have made their sad retreat.

Its facets reflect just as chimes echo chimes,
And in the way a street opens on a street.

Dawn is a kingdom just beyond the world,
Working for us. It lasts for just one instant,
Gritter that greys past, spilling from its tailgate
Daylight. I saw it over and beyond
Swindon, this morning, as the night wore out –
Swindon, part of a dark plain streaked with lilac,
And the dawn just above it, distant kingdom
Pausing towards me, opening its instant,
White bird that passes over with one wingbeat.
Night, that is shut tight, day that is shut tight,
Two closing wardrobe doors and dawn the crack
Always between them where they almost meet –
First and last instant, over and beyond
Swindon, and the night fainting into daylight.

(gimme some truth)

There is no wind, there's no such thing,
the hiss and hurry of the grass
is souls of mice – where else, where else,
where would they go, unshriven, unchurched,
who never crept into a crypt
to shiver prayers, who never slept
through any dumbed-down hip discourse
of doctrine, lifted helium hearts
with worse than Radio 2 upbeats,
top of the popes – who only heard
the trees that are not trees, the stars
that are not stars, the owls that are
not owls, and all the folk of earth
that is not earth, that are not folk?

England. I think some clear and simple thing
eludes me: a small deer, not rare or common,
stepping at dawn through misty pixilations
at the faint edge of an unnamed location.
And my mind sniffs and zigzags, following
too many scents, a heap of diagrams
on blueprint paper, vexing one another,
so I get nowhere – pure mathematician
cracking an egg with far too much precision.
It is quite simple isn't it? The island
sows us and grows us – it can lock us in
a hothouse where a few upstanding flowers
shade out the rest forever, and their children –
or we can sneeze and blow the whole thing open –

Take away their mountain – see them scraping
Along the flat hard ground, blunt crampons.

Take away their corpses, see them racing
Their big black empty cars at the aerodrome.

Take away their thieves, now see them strolling,
Handcuffed together, in the rosegarden.

Take away their ocean, see them clinging
To a park bench in the roar of autumn.

Take away their old age
Take away their children
Take away their laundry
And their planes and coins and see them dancing

In their big boots of air, extravagant
Aristocrats of the Kingdom of Nothing!

This year, as last year, stitchwort, I fear
I am relying on you. Perhaps even more
than I think, perhaps less. If you failed to re-appear,
from the blacked-out hall
where the bulbs sit switched off, wasp-skull small,
in the full fugue of death's orchestra –
if last year's horror, still raw,
the theatres glib, the poetry poor,
the disregard for unwritten law,
made you stay down – would that be the last straw,
the brick that, taken out, brings down the wall?
Or not? I will pass, through all the whistling air,
or stop, and lift your white bell, as before,
with its grey veins, to see what's there.

(Hedges)

What's this great train that slowed across the land
and stopped and put down roots? A web of trains,
in fact, all standing fused on their branch lines.
The dunnock passengers peered out, and wrens,
and here and there a flag of ash was run
up – flag of where? Of general carnival,
with campion flashing in and out, and magpie
Lords of Misrule. The fading destination
festered far-off, the platform spouse or friend
became a sour pine, roots in deeps of sand,
grown very tall with waiting – on one arm,
a single raven of regret. But all
these wagons, leafing out and going nowhere,
are jubilant – they have already got there.

(Scalpay)

To bow down like these hills and pray the light
into my peat – with rocks of strict religion
keeping the sea in place, and at my centre
a Sunday certainty, that knows the scripture
for every nightmare – understands the weather's
long adolescence and the screech of seabirds
as recitation - so the mysteries
run off my back, or sponge into my sphagnum,
by their bright falling deepening the waters
that deepen my repose. Sheep taste the virtue
of my green grace, their lambs suck slowness from them
and bend their heads in worship to the grazing,
and the sun sinks into the place ordained,
and the moon rises, absolute as Amen.

God bless the consonants that call up trees,
For instance, out of frantic waving green,
That bleeds into the blue air with such ease,
If not set out in letters plainly seen
And spoken. Bless the plump and bustling vowels,
Bagged winds or spirits whistling in a box,
Or caged in branches like the cries of owls;
Crying like breezes wincing through sharp rocks.
God bless the indentations, bless the space
Between the words, where the mind glides and drops,
Like a bird over snow without a trace,
Into the cover of the further copse.
God bless apostrophes, like tears that drop
Around a mouth, and God bless the full stop.

(After Dante)

It is so clear, it is so bright a day,
When my sweet lady greets you with a smile,
You have to hide in silence for awhile,
You have to turn your thieving eyes away.
She knows that she is praised but still she goes
Everywhere wrapped in the transparency
Of simple grace, a gentle embassy
From the real world. Hers is the face it shows,
A demonstration given by the sky
To the dark heart so brightly through the eyes,
It cannot be imagined, only known.
An angel made of love is softly blown
Out of her mouth – invisibly it flies
Into the soul, advising it to sigh.

(After Dante)

To every heart locked up in love, who sees
This message I have put into a sonnet,
Which I would like them to reply to please,
With any thoughts that might shed light upon it,
I greet you in the name of Love, your King.
Night was already one third through the hours
The stars are given for their glittering,
When – and remembering that power of powers,
My mouth drops open – Love appeared to me
Suddenly. He was smiling. In his hand
He held my heart, a fire, and my lady
Slept in his arms, wrapped in a mantle, and
He woke her and, priest-like, despite her fears,
Fed her my flames, then ran away in tears.

(Beatrice to Dante)

My love is in the world and I am free.
He walks upon the earth and in the sky
Thinking of him, forgetting him, I fly
Like a white bird where the land meets the sea,
Up to the light, then down into the green,
Or else along the surface like a breeze.
I speak to him of things no eye has seen,
And what I send into his mind, he sees!
I love this game, it is like kite flying,
But if the kite was crackling down the string
The strangest news – what it is like dying,
What it is like to shake off everything
And still be tethered by the trembling thread
Of love between the living and the dead.

Lightning Source UK Ltd.
Milton Keynes UK
UKHW012343210621
385916UK00005B/1437